Crockpot Recipes

56 Delicious Low Sugar Slow Cooker Recipes

A Unique Mix of Recipes To Fit Into Paleo, Mediterranean, Atkins, Dash, Vegetarian & Vegan Diets.

©Copyright Recipe Junkies

All Rights Reserved

Betty AKA Betty Crockpot

Recipe Junkies Alert!

Sign up for Recipe Junkies FREE Newsletter today and never pay more than a buck for a brand new recipe book! Receive alerts about new recipe books before they even come out! You can follow us on Facebook and Twitter as well!

Recipe Junkies Alert Promo

Recipe Junkies Facebook

Recipe Junkies Twitter

For more details email us at ***recipejunkies1@gmail.com***

Contents

Italian Beef Rolls 6

Crust less Spinach and Mushroom Quiche 8

Chile Verde Breakfast Lasagna 10

Eggplant Sauce 12

Chipotle Beef Tacos with Cabbage and Radish Slaw 14

Smoky Slow Cooker Chili 16

Chicken Enchilada Stack 18

Sausage Jambalaya 20

Cabbage Rolls 22

Sweet and Sour Chicken 24

Chickpea Curry 26

Mediterranean Roast Turkey 28

Potato Soup 30

Vegetarian Chili 32

Slow Cooker Spinach Sauce 34

Vegetarian Minestrone 36

Slow Cooker Cassoulet 38

Risotto with Fennel and Barley 40

Slow cooked beans 42

Black Bean and Mushroom Chili 44

Chickpea, Squash and Lentil Stew 46

Chickpea and Eggplant Stew 48

Three Bean and Barley Southern Soup 50

Squash Quinoa Casserole 52

Pinto Bean Sloppy Joe Mix 54

Mexican Spaghetti and Sauce 56

Chicken Soup 58

Slow Cooked Macaroni and Cheese 61

Turkey Stew with Green Chilies 62

Refried Beans 64

Vegetable and Cheese Soup 65

Vegetable and Black Bean Soup 66

Bowtie Pasta and Homemade Tomato Sauce 68

Rice Casserole 70

Potato Soup 71

Split Pea Soup 73

Onion Soup 74

Zucchini Soup 76

German Lentil Soup 78

Meatless Taco Soup 80

Cabbage Soup 82

Corn Chowder 84

Tofu Curry 86

Overnight Oatmeal 88

Sauerkraut soup 90

Lima Bean Soup 92

Vegetarian Minestrone Soup 94

Spicy Thai Soup 96

Lentil and Mushroom Stew 98

Pumpkin Goulash 100

Italian Beef Rolls

Ingredients:

- 1 ½ pound beef brisket
- 2 onions (thinly sliced into rings)
- 2 tbsp corn starch
- Water (desired preference)
- ¼ cup chili sauce
- 1 bay leaf
- ½ tsp dried thyme (crushed)
- 1 garlic clove (minced)
- 10 Italian Bread Rolls

Method:

1. Start by trimming off any excess fat from the beef. Place it in a 6 quart slow cooker along with onions and bay leaf.

2. In a mixing bowl, mix the chili sauce with thyme, salt, pepper and garlic. Combine well and pour it over the meat.

3. Cover the cooker and cook on low heat for approximately 10-12 hours.

4. Once the beef is cooked, transfer it along with the onions onto a serving platter and cover it with a foil.

5.   Next, in a medium sauce pan, pour the remaining mixture and stir it together with cornstarch and water. Cook the mixture for approximately 2 to 3 minutes or until the gravy thickens.

6.   Serve the beef on the Italian rolls and top it off with the gravy.

Nutritional Information:

Calories; 325, Fats 8g, Carbohydrates 35g, Protein 25g

Crustless Spinach and Mushroom Quiche

Ingredients:

- Disposable liner and non stick cooking spray
- 1 package frozen chopped spinach; thawed and drained
- 4 slices bacon
- 1 tablespoon olive oil
- 2 cups Portobello mushrooms; coarsely chopped
- ½ cup sweet red pepper; chopped
- 1 ½ cups grated Swiss cheese
- 8 eggs
- 2 cups whole milk or half and half
- 2 tablespoons fresh chives; snipped
- ½ teaspoon salt
- ½ teaspoon black pepper
- ½ cup biscuit mix

Method:

1. Line the slow cooker and spray liner with non stick spray.

2. Cook bacon until crisp; drain and crumble.

3. Heat olive oil and add mushrooms and pepper. Cook until tender then add spinach and cheese.

4. Combine eggs, milk, chives, salt, and pepper and stir into spinach mixture. Add the biscuit mixture and gently fold. Pour into slow cooker and sprinkle with prepared bacon crumbs.

5. Cook in slow cooker on low for 4 to 5 hours. If using high heat cook for 2 to 2.5 hours. Cool 15 to 30 minutes before serving.

Nutritional Information:

Calories; 431, Fats 31g, Carbohydrates 66g, Protein 25g, Sugar 2g

Chile Verde Breakfast Lasagna

Ingredients:

- 1 pound bulk breakfast sausage
- ¾ cup chopped sweet green pepper; finely chopped
- 1 jalapeno pepper; stemmed, seeded, and finely chopped
- 5 eggs beaten lightly
- 2 teaspoons vegetable oil
- ¼ cup green onions; sliced
- ¼ snipped cilantro or parsley
- ½ teaspoon salt
- ½ teaspoon cumin
- 9 corn tortillas; 6 inch
- 2 cups Monterey jack cheese; shredded
- 1 16 ounce jar green salsa

Method:

1. Lightly coat the inside of the slow cooker with non stick cooking spray.

2. Brown sausage in skillet and drain off fat. Add the sweet pepper and jalapeno pepper to skillet and cook over medium heat for 1 minute. Transfer sausage and peppers to bowl.

3. In the same pan cook eggs in hot oil just until set; stir to break up eggs. Combine eggs with sausage and peppers. Stir in green onions, cilantro, salt, and cumin.

4. Place 3 of the tortillas in the bottom of the slow cooker; it is fine if they over lap. Put half the egg and sausage mixture in the slow cooker and sprinkle with ½ cup of the cheese.

1. Pour 2/3 of the salsa over the mixture in slow cooker. Continue layering until all tortillas, sausage mixture, and salsa are in slow cooker.

5. Cover and set to low heat for 3 to 4 hours. Let stand for 15 minute before serving. Can top with sour cream and cilantro if desired.

Nutritional Information:

Calories; 429, Fats 29g, Carbohydrates 18g, Protein 21g, Sugar 3g

Eggplant Sauce

Ingredients:

- 1 eggplant
- 2 14.5 oz. cans diced tomatoes
- 6 oz. tomato paste (canned)
- 1 4 oz. can sliced mushrooms; drained
- ¼ cup red wine (optional)
- ¼ cup water
- ½ cup onion (chopped)
- 2 cloves of garlic (chopped)
- 1 ½ teaspoon oregano
- 1/3 cup olives (pitted)
- 2 tablespoons fresh parsley; chopped
- Black pepper
- Parmesan cheese (shredded; optional)

Method:

1. Peel eggplant and cut into small cubes

2. In the slow cooker combine the eggplant, onion, canned tomatoes with juice, tomato paste, mushrooms, wine, water, garlic, and oregano.

3. Cover the slow cooker and allow it to cook on low heat for approximately 7 to 8 hours.

4. Add the olives and parsley.

6. Serve over cooked noodles and sprinkle with Parmesan cheese.

Nutritional Information:

Calories; 346, Fats 4g, Carbohydrates 65g, Protein 13g, Sugar 5g

Chipotle Beef Tacos with Cabbage and Radish Slaw

Ingredients:

- 3 pounds beef; trimmed and cut into 2 inch cubes
- 1 large onion; sliced thin
- 4 chopped cloves of garlic
- 1 to 3 tablespoons chopped chipotle; canned in adobo sauce
- 1 teaspoon oregano
- 2 bay leaves
- Kosher salt
- 4 cups cabbage; thinly sliced
- 4 radishes (halved and thinly sliced)
- ¼ cup fresh cilantro
- 2 tablespoons lime juice
- Corn tortillas
- Toppings: sour cream, salsa, jalapenos, shredded cheese

Method:

1. In the slow cooker toss together the beef, garlic, onion, chipotles, oregano, bay leaves, and salt. (tip: add just a bit of water to bottom to avoid sticking)

2. Cook on high for 3.5 to 4 hour or on low for 7 to 8 hours.

3. Twenty minutes before meat mixture is done wrap tortillas in foil and place in 350 degree oven for 5 to ten minutes to warm.

4. While tortillas are warming and meat is finishing up, toss together the cabbage, radishes, lime juice, and ¼ teaspoon salt.

5. Transfer the meat to a bowl and shred with a fork; save the broth. Strain the liquid into the meat and stir to combine.

6. Fill tortillas with beef and slaw; top with your choice of toppings.

Nutritional Information:

Calories; 521, Fats 6g, Carbohydrates 34g, Protein 57g, Sugar 5g

Smoky Slow Cooker Chili

Ingredients:

- 1 pound ground pork
- 1 pound pork shoulder; trimmed and cut into ½ inch cubes
- 1 ¾ cup bell pepper; chopped
- 3 cups chopped onion
- 3 minced cloves of garlic
- 3 tablespoons tomato paste
- 3 tablespoons chili powder
- 1 tablespoon cumin
- 2 teaspoons oregano
- ¾ teaspoon black pepper
- 6 quarter tomatillos
- 2 bay leaves
- 2 14.5 oz. cans plum tomatoes; chopped and drained
- 1 15 oz. can pinto beans drained; no salt added
- 1 7.75 oz. can Mexican style tomato sauce
- 1 smoked ham hock
- ½ cup cilantro; chopped finely
- ½ cup green onion; chopped finely
- ½ cup crumbled queso fresco

- 8 lime wedges

Method:

1. Brown pork in skillet and transfer to slow cooker after draining fat.

2. Brown pork should pieces in skillet until browned and transfer to slow cooker after draining fat.

3. In skill sprayed with non stick spray sauté onion and pepper for 8 minutes; stirring often. Add garlic and sauté 1 minute more. Add tomato paste and cook for 1 minute; stirring constantly. Add onion mixture to slow cooker with meat.

4. Add chili powder, cumin, pepper, tomatillos, bay leaves, plum tomatoes, beans, tomato sauce, and ham hock. Cover and set slow cooker on high for 5 hours.

5. Remove bay leaves and ham hock; discard.

6. Ladle into serving cups or bowls; top with 1 tablespoon cilantro, cheese, green onions, and serve with a lime wedge.

Nutritional Information:

Calories; 357, Fats 14.4g, Carbohydrates 26g, Protein 27.7g

Chicken Enchilada Stack

Ingredients:

- 1 teaspoon canola oil
- 1 cup onion; chopped
- ½ cup poblano, seeded and chopped
- 2 minced cloves garlic
- 1 ½ teaspoon chipotle chili powder
- 1 14.5 oz. diced tomatoes; drained and no salt added
- 1 8 oz. canned tomato sauce; Italian seasoned
- Cooking spray
- 2 cups rotisserie chicken breast; shredded
- 1 cup frozen; white and yellow corn
- 1 15 oz. can black beans; drained and rinsed
- 5 corn and flour tortillas
- 8 oz. shredded cheddar cheese; reduced fat
- Cilantro sprigs

Method:

1. 1.Using a nonstick skillet heat on medium and add oil. Add onion, pepper, and garlic; cook until tender; about 6 minutes.

2.   Stir in chili powder, tomatoes, and tomato sauce. Put half the tomato mixture in a blender. Remove lid of blender and let steam escape. Place a towel over blender and blend until almost smooth and pour into a bowl. Repeat process with the other half of tomato mixture.

3.   Spray slow cooker with non stick cooking spray. Spread 3 tablespoons of tomato mixture on bottom of slow cooker. Mix the remainder of tomato mixture with chicken, corn, and beans.

4.   Place one tortilla on the tomato mixture in slow cooker. Cover with 1 cup of chicken mixture. Sprinkle with cheese; about 1/3 cup. Top with another tortilla and repeat process until all tortillas and chicken mixture are in slow cooker.

5.   Cook on low setting for 2 hours or until the cheese is melted and the edges are browned.

Nutritional Information:

Calories; 295, Fats 10.3g, Carbohydrates 16g, Protein 24g

Sausage Jambalaya

Ingredients:

- 2 cups onions; chopped
- 1 cup celery; chopped
- 1 cup water
- ½ teaspoon Cajun season
- ½ teaspoon thyme dried
- 1 pound skinless chicken (breast or thighs) cut into 1" cubes
- 8 ounces sausage sliced
- 4 cups cooked rice
- 1 14 oz canned tomatoes (diced with green chilies) undrained
- 1 pound medium size shrimp; peeled and deveined
- 4 cups cooked rice

Method:

1. Combine the first 8 ingredients in slow cooker; cover and cook on low for 6 hours.

2. Stir in shrimp and cook 10 minutes longer on low or until shrimp is done.

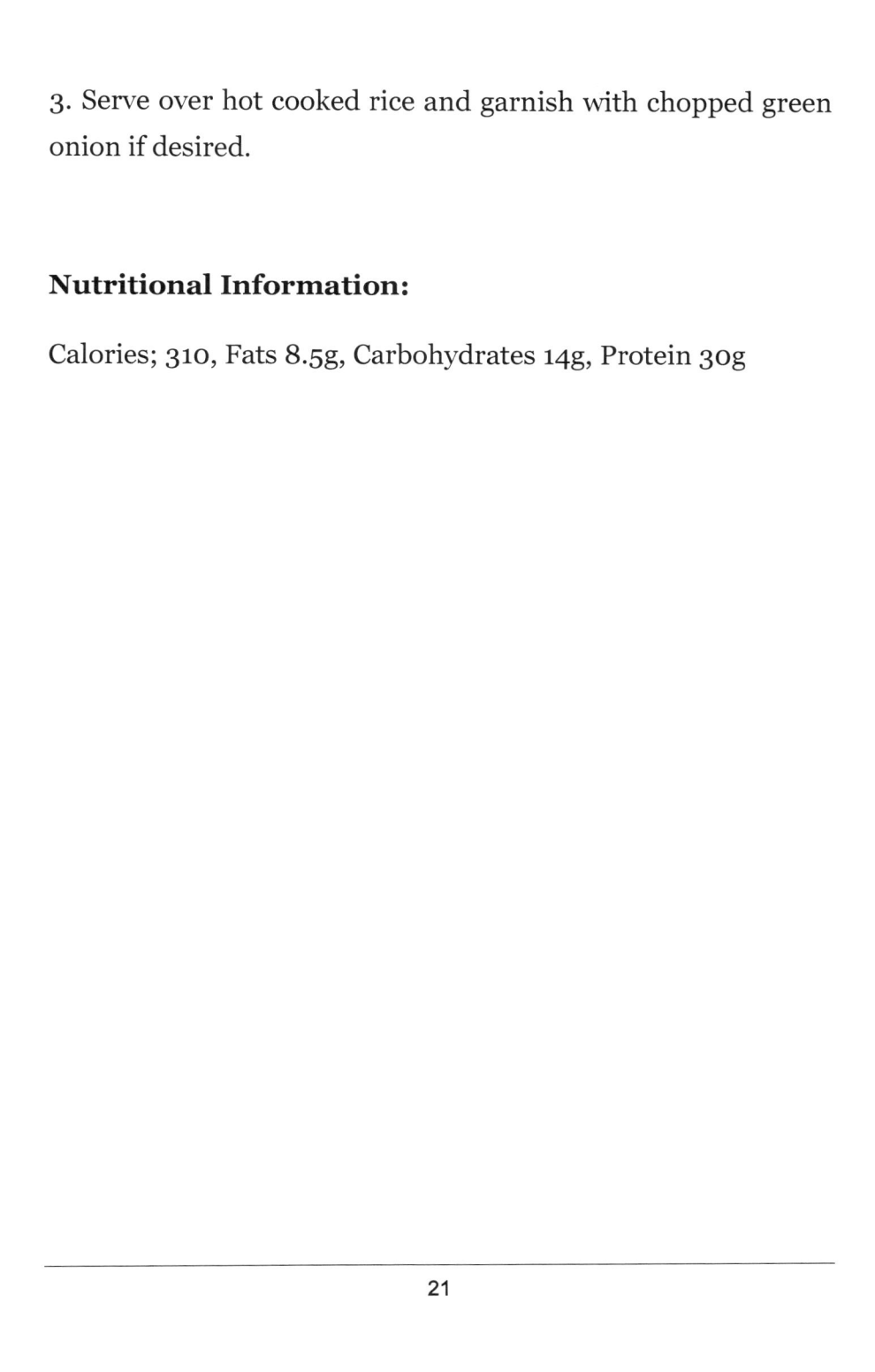

3. Serve over hot cooked rice and garnish with chopped green onion if desired.

Nutritional Information:

Calories; 310, Fats 8.5g, Carbohydrates 14g, Protein 30g

Cabbage Rolls

Ingredients:

- 12 large cabbage leaves
- 3 cups onion; chopped
- ½ cup instant rice; uncooked
- ½ pound ground pork; lean
- ½ pound pork breakfast sausage; 50% lean
- ¼ teaspoon black pepper
- 1 14.4 oz. can sauerkraut; shredded; drained and rinsed
- ½ teaspoon caraway seeds
- 2 cups tomato juice; low sodium
- 2 tablespoon brown sugar light (optional)
- 3 tablespoons tomato paste

Method:

1. Cook cabbage leaves in boiling water until tender; about 3 to 4 minutes.

2. Sauté onion in skillet for 5 to 7 minutes or until tender; add rice stir and let stand for 15 minutes.

3. Combine rice, pork, and pepper. Fill cabbage leaf with about ¼ cup meat mixture and turn sides in and roll. Repeat for all cabbage leaves.

4. Mix caraway seed with sauerkraut. Put half the sauerkraut mixture into bottom of slow cooker after coating with non stick spray. Top layer of sauerkraut with half the cabbage rolls. Repeat this step with remaining sauerkraut and cabbage rolls.

5. Combine tomato juice, brown sugar, and tomato paste with a whisk. Pour tomato juice mixture over sauerkraut and cabbage rolls. Cook on low setting for 6 hours and serve.

Nutritional Information:

Calories; 287, Fats 10.8g, Carbohydrates 12.3g, Protein 17.7g

Sweet and Sour Chicken

Ingredients:

- 1 cup onion; chopped
- 1/3 cup sugar
- 1/3 cup ketchup
- ¼ orange juice
- 3 tablespoons cider vinegar
- 2 tablespoons soy sauce; low sodium
- 1 tablespoon grated fresh ginger
- 1 pound skinless chicken (cubed)
- 2 cans pineapple chunks; 8 ounce
- 1 bell pepper; large, cut into ¾ inch pieces
- 1 red pepper; large cut into ¾ inch pieces
- 3 cups cooked rice

Method:

1. Combine the first 12 ingredients in a slow cooker.
2. Cook on high for 4 hours or 6 hours on low covered.
3. Serve over hot brown rice.

Nutritional Information:

Calories; 332, Fats 3.4g, Carbohydrates 7.1g, Protein 18.4g

Chickpea Curry

Ingredients:

- 2 cups cauliflower florets; small
- 2 cups peeled and cubed sweet potato
- 1 cup onion; chopped
- 1 tablespoon curry powder
- 1 tablespoon grated ginger; grated
- 1 ¼ teaspoon salt
- 2 minced garlic cloves
- 1 can chickpeas; drained and rinsed (16 oz.)
- 1 can no salt diced tomatoes; un-drained (14.5 oz.)
- 1 can coconut milk (light) (13.5oz)
- 1 package extra-firm tofu; drained (14 oz.)
- 1 tablespoon canola oil
- 3 cups cooked rice
- 3 tablespoons chopped cilantro; fresh

Method:

1. Combine first 11 ingredients in slow cooker and stir well. Cover and cook on low setting for 5.5 hours or until vegetables are tender.

2. Place tofu on layers of paper towels and cover with additional towels. Press down to absorb excess liquid and cut into ½ cubes.

3. Heat oil in pan and cook tofu for 8 to 10 minutes or until browned. Stir into mixture in slow cooker.'

4. Serve over rice and garnish with cilantro.

Nutritional Information:

Calories; 328, Fats 7g, Carbohydrates 11g, Protein 12.8g

Mediterranean Roast Turkey

Ingredients:

- 2 cups onion; chopped
- ½ cup pitted olives
- ½ cup Julienne-cut and drained oil packed tomato halves sun dried
- 2 tablespoons lemon juice
- 1 ½ teaspoon garlic minced
- 1 teaspoon Greek seasoning mix
- ½ teaspoon salt
- ¼ teaspoon pepper
- 1 trimmed turkey breast (4 pounds)
- ½ cup fat free chicken brother; low sodium
- 3 tablespoons all purpose flour
- Thyme sprigs

Method:

1. Put first 9 ingredients in slow cooker. Add ¼ cup chicken broth, cover and cook for 7 hours on low.

2. Whisk the remaining flour and chicken broth and pour into slow cooker. Cook for an additional 30 minutes on low setting.

Nutritional Information:

Calories; 314, Fats 4.9g, Carbohydrates 16.2g, Protein 57g

Potato Soup

Ingredients:

- 3 slices bacon
- 1 cup onion; chopped
- 3 pounds potatoes; peeled and cut into ¼ thick slices
- ½ cup water
- 2 cans chicken broth; low sodium and reduced fat
- ½ teaspoon salt
- ½ teaspoon black pepper
- 2 cups low fat milk
- 4 oz. reduced fat cheddar cheese; shredded
- ½ cup sour cream (light)
- 4 teaspoons chopped chives

Method:

1. Cook bacon in skillet until crisp. Remove bacon from pan and add onion to drippings. Sauté for 3 minutes.

2. Put potato slices and onion in slow cooker after coating with non stick spray. Combine water with the next three ingredients and add to slow cooker. Cover and cook on low heat for 8 hours or until potatoes are tender.

3. Mash mixture with a potato masher. Stir in milk and ¾ cup cheese. Turn heat to high and cook for 20 minutes.

4. Serve in bowls topped with sour cream, chive, and crumbled bacon.

Nutritional Information:

Calories; 259, Fats 6.4g, Carbohydrates 9g, Protein 13.2g

Vegetarian Chili

Ingredients:

- 14 ounce can of firm tofu (drained and cubed)
- 15.5 ounce canned black beans (drained)
- 15 ounce canned tomatoes (crushed)
- 4 onions (chopped)
- 2 red bell peppers (seeded and chopped)
- 2 green bell peppers (seeded and chopped)
- 4 cloves of garlic
- 2 tsp ground cumin
- ½ tsp ground black pepper
- 6 tbsp chili powder
- 2 tbsp dried oregano
- 2 tsp salt
- 2 tbsp white vinegar (distilled)
- 1 tbsp hot pepper sauce
- ½ cup olive oil (extra virgin)

Method:

1. In a large skillet, heat the oil over medium heat.

2.	Add the onions to it and cook until softened. Next add in the peppers, tofu and garlic and cook for approximately for ten minutes or until the vegetables start to turn brown and tender.

3.	Now cook the beans in a slow cooker over low heat. Stir in all the vegetables and tomatoes and season it.

4.	Cover and cook for approximately six to eight hours.

Nutritional Information:

Calories; 445, Fats 18.2g, Carbohydrates 58.2g, Protein 21.2g

Slow Cooker Spinach Sauce

Ingredients:

- 28 ounce canned tomatoes (peeled and crushed)
- 10 ounce frozen spinach (chopped, thawed and drained)
- 1 onion (chopped)
- 1/3 cup carrot (grated)
- 2 ½ tbsp red pepper (crushed)
- 5 garlic cloves (minced)
- 6 ounce canned tomato paste
- 4.5 ounce canned mushrooms (sliced and drained)
- 2 tbsp dried oregano
- 2 tsp salt
- 2 tbsp dried basil
- 2 bay leaves
- ¼ cup olive oil (extra virgin)

Method:

1. Combine olive oil with spinach, onion, garlic, carrots, tomato paste and mushrooms in a 5 quart slow cooker.

2. Add in the salt, pepper, oregano, bay leaves and tomatoes.

3.   Cover and cook for approximately 4 hours over high heat. After 4 hours are up, stir and reduce the heat to low and cook for an additional 2 hours.

Nutritional Information:

Calories; 176, Fats 8.2g, Carbohydrates 25.1g, Protein 6.6g

Vegetarian Minestrone

Ingredients:

- 6 cups vegetable broth
- 15 ounce canned kidney beans (drained)
- 28 ounce canned tomatoes (crushed)
- 4 cups spinach (freshly chopped)
- 1 onion (chopped)
- 2 large carrots (diced)
- 2 celery ribs (diced)
- 1 zucchini
- 1 cup green beans
- 1 tbsp parsley (minced)
- 3 garlic cloves (minced)
- ¾ tsp thyme (dried)
- 1 ½ tsp oregano (dried)
- 1 tsp salt
- 1/3 tsp ground black pepper
- ½ cup elbow macaroni (cooked)
- ¼ cup Parmesan cheese (finely grated)

Method:

1. In a 6 quart slow cooker, combine the vegetable broth with kidney beans, green beans, tomatoes, onion, zucchini, celery and carrot.

2. Season it with garlic, thyme, parsley, oregano, salt and black pepper.

3. Cook the minestrone on low heat for approximately 7 to 8 hours.

4. Next, stir the spinach and macaroni into the minestrone and allow it to cook for another 15 minutes or so.

5. Top it off with grated Parmesan cheese.

Nutritional Information:

Calories; 138, Fats 1.7g, Carbohydrates 25.2g, Protein 6.9g

Slow Cooker Cassoulet

Ingredients:

- 1 pound navy beans (dry; soaked overnight)
- 4 cups mushroom broth
- 1 cube vegetable bouillon
- 1 onion
- 2 carrots (peeled and diced)
- 1 potato (peeled and cubed)
- 4 sprigs of parsley
- 1 sprig of rosemary
- 1 sprig of lemon thyme (chopped)
- 1 sprig of savory
- 1 bay leaf
- 2 tbsp olive oil (extra virgin)

Method:

1. In a large skillet, heat the oil over medium heat. Stir in the onion and the carrots and cook until it becomes tender.

2. In a slow cooker, combine the beans with the broth, bouillon, carrots, onion and bay leaf. Add in half a cup of water if required.

3. Season the mixture with parsley, thyme, rosemary and savory and allow it to cook on low heat for approximately 8 hours or so.

4. Next, stir in the potato and continue to cook for another hour.

5. Remove all the herbs and serve!

Nutritional Information:

Calories; 279, Fats 4.4g, Carbohydrates 47.2g, Protein 15.3g

Risotto with Fennel and Barley

Ingredients:

- 2 teaspoons of fennel seeds
- 1 fennel bulb, cored and diced
- 1 cup of brown rice
- 1 carrot, chopped
- 1 shallot, chopped
- 2 cloves of garlic, minced
- 4 cups of chicken broth
- 1 ½ cups of water
- 1/3 cup of dry white wine(optional)
- 2 cups of green beans
- ½ cup of shredded parmesan cheese
- 1/3 cup of pitted black olives, chopped
- 1 tablespoon of grated lemon zest
- ½ teaspoon of salt
- ½ teaspoon of pepper

Method:

1. Chop the carrot, the shallot, the black olives and core and chop the fennel bulb

2.	Grate the lemon zest and mince the garlic

3.	Place all of the ingredients into the slow cooker and stir until well mixed

4.	Cook for three and a half hours on low

5.	Stir and cook until desired heat is cooked all the way through

6.	Serve and enjoy, try some parmesan cheese on top

Nutritional Information:

Calories: 242 kcal, Fats: 6 grams, Carbohydrates: 36 grams, Protein: 10 grams

Slow cooked beans

Ingredients:

- 1 pound of dried beans, mix pinto beans with black beans and kidney beans
- 1 onion, chopped
- 4 cloves of garlic, minced
- 1 teaspoon of thyme
- 1 bay leaf
- 5 cups of boiling water
- ½ teaspoon of salt

Method:

1. Place the beans in a large pot with the water, bring to a boil on high heat and cook for about one hour

2. Drain the beans

3. Chop the onion and mince the garlic

4. Add to the beans and stir well

5. Lower heat and cook for about three more hours

6. Add the salt and cook for 15 more minutes

7. Serve and enjoy

Nutritional Information:

Calories: 260 kcal, Fats: 1 gram, Carbohydrates: 48 grams, Protein: 15 grams

Black Bean and Mushroom Chili

Ingredients:

- 1 pound of black beans
- 1 tablespoon of extra virgin olive oil
- ¼ cup of mustard seeds
- 2 tablespoons of chili powder
- 1 ½ teaspoons of cumin
- ½ teaspoon of cardamom
- 2 onions, chopped
- 1 pound of mushrooms, chopped
- 8 ounces of tomatillos, husk them and rinse and chop
- ¼ cup of water
- 5 ½ cups of mushroom broth
- 1 6-ounce can of tomato paste
- 2 tablespoons of minced garlic
- 1 ¼ cups of pepper jack cheese
- ½ cup of sour cream
- ½ cup of cilantro
- 2 limes cut into wedges

Method:

1. Place the beans in a large pot with water and boil on medium to high heat for about an hour

2. Drain and mix in the rest of the ingredients in a Dutch oven

3. Cook on low to medium heat for about five hours

4. Serve and enjoy, try with some sour cream and shredded cheese

Nutritional Information:

Calories: 306 kcal, Fats: 10 grams, Carbohydrates: 40 grams, Protein: 18 grams

Chickpea, Squash and Lentil Stew

Ingredients:

- ¾ cup of chickpeas
- 2 ½ pounds of squash, peeled and cut into chunks
- 2 carrots, peeled and sliced
- 1 onion, chopped
- 1 cup of red lentils
- 4 cups of vegetable broth
- 2 tablespoons of tomato paste
- 1 tablespoon of ginger, minced
- 1 ½ teaspoons of cumin
- 1 teaspoon of salt
- ¼ teaspoon of saffron
- ¼ teaspoon of pepper
- ¼ cup of lime juice
- ½ cup of peanuts, chopped
- ¼ cup of cilantro

Method:

1. Place the beans in a large crock pot and bring to a boil, cook for about an hour

2. Drain and combine everything but the peanuts and the cilantro in the slow cooker

3. Cook on low for about five hours

4. Serve and enjoy, sprinkle with cilantro and peanuts

Nutritional Information:

Calories: 294 kcal, Fats: 7 grams, Carbohydrates: 48 grams, Protein: 14 grams

Chickpea and Eggplant Stew

Ingredients:

- 1 cup of mushrooms
- 3 cups of water
- 2 eggplants, peeled and cut
- 3 tablespoons of olive oil
- 2 onions, sliced
- 6 cloves of garlic, minced
- 2 teaspoons of oregano
- 1 cinnamon stick
- 1 teaspoon of salt
- 1 teaspoon of pepper
- 1 bay leaf
- 1 cup of dried chickpeas
- 3 tomatoes, chopped
- ¼ cup of parsley

Method:

1. Preheat the oven to 400 degrees

2. Peel and cut the eggplants, cut the mushrooms and everything else that needs to be cut

3. Place on baking sheet and cook for 6 minutes

4. Then transfer to the slow cooker

5. Cook for four hours on high

6. Remove the cinnamon stick and the bay leaf

7. Serve and enjoy

Nutritional Information:

Calories: 219 kcal, Fats: 7 rams, Carbohydrates: 33 grams, Protein: 9 grams

Three Bean and Barley Southern Soup

Ingredients:

- 1 tablespoon of olive oil
- 1 onion, diced
- 1 stalk of celery, diced
- 1 carrot, diced
- 9 cups of water
- 4 cups of vegetable broth
- ½ cup of pearl barley
- 1/3 cup of black beans
- 1/3 cup of great northern beans
- 1/3 cup of kidney beans
- 1 tablespoon of chili powder
- 1 teaspoon of cumin
- ½ teaspoon of oregano
- ¾ teaspoon of salt

Method:

1. Cut everything up that needs to be cut and mix it all together in the Dutch oven

2.   Put on low heat and cook for about two and a half hours

3.   Serve and enjoy

Nutritional Information:

Calories: 205 kcal, Fats: 3 grams, Carbohydrates: 35 grams, Protein: 11 grams

Squash Quinoa Casserole

Ingredients:

- 12 ounces of tomatillos, de-husked and chopped
- 1 pint of cherry tomatoes, chopped
- 1 bell pepper, chopped
- ½ cup of chopped onion
- 1 tablespoon of lime juice
- 1 teaspoon of salt
- 1 cup of quinoa
- 1 cup of feta cheese
- 2 pounds of yellow squash, sliced
- 2 tablespoons of oregano

Method:

1. Chop everything up that needs to get cut

2. Place everything in the slow cooker and cook on low for four hours

3. Serve and enjoy

Nutritional Information:

Calories: 111 kcal, Fats: 3 grams, Carbohydrates: 18 grams, Protein: 5 grams

Pinto Bean Sloppy Joe Mix

Ingredients:

- 2 tablespoons of olive oil
- 2 carrots, sliced
- 1 onion, sliced
- 4 cloves of garlic, minced
- 3 tablespoons of chili powder
- 2 tablespoons of balsamic vinegar
- 1 cup of pinto beans
- 1 red bell pepper, diced
- 8 ounces of tomato sauce
- ½ cup of water
- 2 tablespoons of soy sauce
- 2 tablespoons of tomato paste
- 4 cups of green cabbage, sliced
- 1 zucchini, chopped
- 1 cup of corn
- 3 tablespoons of honey mustard
- 1 teaspoon of salt
- 10 whole wheat hamburger buns

Method:

1. Cut up everything that needs to get cut up and place in slow cooker

2. Cook on high heat for 5 hours with the other ingredients

3. Place the cabbage and the zucchini in the last 30 minutes

4. Serve on buns and enjoy

Nutritional Information:

Calories: 283 kcal, Fats: 6 grams, Carbohydrates: 51 grams, Protein: 11 grams

Mexican Spaghetti and Sauce

Ingredients:

- 1 cup of chopped onion
- 1 tablespoon of olive oil
- 4 cups of meatless spaghetti sauce
- 1 can of black beans
- 1 cup of diced tomatoes
- 1 cup of corn
- ¼ cup of salsa
- 4 ounces of green chilies
- 1 tablespoon of chili powder
- ¼ teaspoon of pepper
- 1 box of spaghetti

Method:

1. Chop the onion up and cook in a skillet with the oil until they are clear

2. In a large saucepan combine everything else together and stir well

3. Cook on a simmer for about 20 minutes

4.   Serve sauce over spaghetti noodles and enjoy

Nutritional Information:

Calories: 216.3 kcal, Fats: 4.8 grams, Carbohydrates: 36.1 grams, Protein: 9.0 grams

Chicken Soup

Ingredients:

- 3-4 chicken breasts
- 8 cloves fresh garlic, chopped
- Low salt and freshly ground pepper, to taste
- 2 heaping cups cabbage (thinly shredded)
- 1 green bell pepper (deseeded, diced)
- 1 yellow summer squash (diced)
- 2 zucchini squash, cut up
- 6 to 8 baby potatoes cut up
- 1 4-oz. can chopped green chillies
- 1 tsp sage
- 1 tsp each of: dried basil, oregano, and parsley
- 1 14-oz. can diced tomatoes
- 2 or more cups chicken broth, as needed
- A dash or two of balsamic vinegar to taste
- Olive oil, as needed

Method:

1. Drizzle some olive oil into a slow cooker and lay the chicken breasts in it, with half the chopped garlic. Season a little with sea salt and pepper.

2. In a bowl, combine the bell pepper, shredded cabbage, zucchini squashes, potatoes, and green chilies, tossing them with another drizzle of olive oil. Season the mixture with sea salt, black pepper, herbs and toss to coat.

3. Pour the veggie mix into the slow cooker in an even layer. Add in the tomatoes, chicken broth, and a small dash of balsamic vinegar, to taste.

4. The liquid content should just about cover the veggies in the pot. If you like, you can add more broth to get better consistency of a soup.

5. Cover the pot and let it cook for up to 5 to 6 hours, or until the chicken is tender and easily breaks apart into pieces.

Nutritional Information:

Calories: 277 kcal; Fats: 8.9g; Carbohydrates: 13.6g; Protein: 35.0g

Slow Cooked Macaroni and Cheese

Ingredients:

- 2 eggs
- 1 ½ cups of milk
- 12 ounces of evaporated milk
- ½ pound of elbow macaroni
- 4 cups of shredded cheddar cheese
- 1 teaspoon of salt
- ½ teaspoon of pepper

Method:

1. Combine everything into the slow cooker and stir well
2. Cook on low for about five hours and stir every so often
3. Serve and enjoy

Nutritional Information:

Calories: 592 kcal, Fats: 33.5 grams, Carbohydrates: 39.5 grams, Protein: 32.6 grams

Turkey Stew with Green Chilies

Ingredients:

- 1 ½ cups butternut squash (peeled and diced)
- 1 lb. ground turkey
- 1 large potatoe (optional & diced)
- 3 medium carrots (peeled and chopped)
- 1 onion (diced)
- 4 cloves garlic (minced)
- 1 tsp cumin
- 1 tsp chili powder
- 1 cup roasted chopped green chili
- 1 quart chicken stock
- Low salt and black pepper to taste

For serving:

- Juice from 1 lime
- 2-3 tbsp chopped cilantro

- 1-2 tsp agave nectar, as needed

Method:

1. Firstly, brown the ground pork in a skillet and take out the excess fat, if any.

2. Now add the pork to the slow cooker with the remaining ingredients up to sea salt and black pepper. Stir well to combine.

3. Cover and cook until the pork is done.

4. About 20 minutes before serving, stir in the lime juice and cilantro. Add some sweetener, if needed, to balance out the spice and if you need a little more liquid, add more broth to it and heat through.

Nutritional information:

Calories: 423 kcal; Fats: 13.5g; Carbohydrates: 44.7g; Protein: 36.3g

Refried Beans

Ingredients:

- 1 onion, chopped
- 3 cups of pinto beans
- ¼ cup of chopped jalapeno pepper
- 2 tablespoons of minced garlic
- 5 teaspoons of salt
- ¾ teaspoons of pepper
- 1/8 teaspoon of cumin
- 9 cups of water

Method:

1. Chop up the onion and place in the slow cooker with everything else

2. Cook on high for about five hours

3. Once the beans are cooked, strain them and mash them

4. Serve and enjoy

Nutritional Information:

Calories: 139 kcal, Fats: 0.5 grams, Carbohydrates: 25.4 grams, Protein: 8.5 grams

Vegetable and Cheese Soup

Ingredients:

- 3 cups of creamed corn
- 1 cup of potatoes, peeled and cubed
- 1 cup of carrots, chopped
- ½ onion, chopped
- 1 teaspoon of celery seed
- ½ teaspoon of pepper
- 6 cups of vegetable broth
- 3 cups of cheese sauce

Method:

1. Peel and chop everything then place in the slow cooker
2. Stir well and cook on medium heat for about five hours
3. Serve and enjoy

Nutritional Information:

Calories: 316 kcal, Fats: 16.5 grams, Carbohydrates: 32.1 grams, Protein: 11.9 grams

Vegetable and Black Bean Soup

Ingredients:

- 1 pound of black beans
- 1 ½ quarts of water
- 1 carrot, chopped
- 1 stalk of celery, chopped
- 1 red onion, chopped
- 6 cloves of garlic, crushed
- 2 green bell peppers, chopped
- 2 jalapeno peppers, chopped
- ¼ cup of lentils
- 4 diced tomatoes
- 2 tablespoons of chili powder
- 2 teaspoons of ground cumin
- ½ teaspoon of oregano
- ½ teaspoon of pepper
- 1 tablespoon of salt
- ½ cup of white rice

Method:

1. Chop and mince everything and them mix it all together in the slow cooker

2. Place on high heat and cook for about three hours

3. Serve and enjoy

Nutritional Information:

Calories: 231 kcal, Fats: 1.2 grams, Carbohydrates: 43.4 grams, Protein: 12.6 grams

Bowtie Pasta and Homemade Tomato Sauce

Ingredients:

- 10 plum tomatoes, peeled and crushed
- ½ of an onion, chopped
- 1 teaspoon of garlic, minced
- ¼ cup of olive oil
- 1 teaspoon of oregano
- 1 teaspoon of basil
- 1 teaspoon of cayenne pepper
- 1 teaspoon of salt
- 1 teaspoon of pepper
- 1 pinch of cinnamon
- 1 box of bowtie pasta

Method:

1. Peel and crush the tomatoes, mince the garlic and chop the onion

2. Place everything in the slow cooker and stir well

3. Cook on high for about four hours or so

4. Serve and enjoy

Nutritional Information:

Calories: 105 kcal, Fats: 9.3 grams, Carbohydrates: 5.5 grams, Protein: 1.2 grams

Rice Casserole

Ingredients:

- 2 onions, chopped
- 3 stalks of celery, sliced
- 4 ½ cups of mixed rice
- 2 ½ cups of water
- 1 can of mushroom soup
- ½ cup of butter
- ½ pound of shredded American cheese
- ½ cup of mushrooms, sliced

Method:

1. Chop everything up that needs to get cut and place in the slow cooker

2. Add everything else but the cheese in the slow cooker

3. Cook on high for about four hours

4. Serve and enjoy with the shredded cheese on top

Nutritional Information:

Calories: 408 kcal, Fats: 23 grams, Carbohydrates: 39.5 grams, Protein: 11.6 grams

Potato Soup

Ingredients:

- 1 onion, chopped
- 4 cups of chicken broth
- 2 cups of water
- 5 potatoes, diced
- ½ teaspoon of salt
- ½ teaspoon of dill weed
- ½ teaspoon of pepper
- ½ cup of all-purpose flour
- 2 cups of half and half cream
- 12 ounces of evaporated milk

Method:

1. Chop and dice everything that needs to get cut and combine all of the ingredients into the slow cooker

2. Cook on high heat for about three and a half hours

3. Serve and enjoy, try with some sour cream and some shredded cheese on top

Nutritional Information:

Calories: 553 kcal, Fats: 19.3 grams, Carbohydrates: 74.2 grams, Protein: 22 grams

Split Pea Soup

Ingredients:

- 1 pound of split peas
- 1 onion, chopped
- 3 carrots, chopped
- 3 stalks of celery, chopped
- 2 cloves of garlic, minced
- 1/8 teaspoon of pepper
- 1 pinch of red pepper flakes
- 8 cups of chicken broth

Method:

1. Chop everything up that needs to get cut and place all of the ingredients into the slow cooker

2. Cook on high heat for about five hours, stirring every so often

3. Serve and enjoy

Nutritional Information:

Calories: 273 kcal, Fats: 3.4 grams, Carbohydrates: 44 grams, Protein: 17.7 grams

Onion Soup

Ingredients:

- 6 tablespoons of butter
- 4 onions, sliced
- 2 cloves of garlic, minced
- ½ cup of cooking sherry
- 7 cups of vegetable broth
- 1 teaspoon of salt
- ¼ teaspoon of thyme
- 1 bay leaf
- 8 slices of French bread
- ½ cup of shredded parmesan cheese
- 1/3 cup of shredded Colby jack cheese
- ¼ cup of cheddar cheese
- 2 tablespoons of mozzarella cheese

Method:

1. Chop everything up that needs to be cut and place in the slow cooker

2. Add in everything else but the cheese and the bread

3. Broil the bread in the oven for about three months

4.   Place the slow cooker on high heat and cook for five hours

5.   Serve and enjoy with some of the bread and the cheese on top

Nutritional Information:

Calories: 250 kcal, Fats: 14.7 grams, Carbohydrates: 17.5 grams, Protein: 11 grams

Zucchini Soup

Ingredients:

- 2 cups of chopped celery
- 2 pounds of zucchini, sliced
- 6 tomatoes, diced
- 2 green bell peppers, sliced
- 1 cup of chopped onion
- 2 teaspoons of salt
- 1 teaspoon of oregano
- 1 teaspoon of Italian seasoning
- 1 teaspoon of basil
- ¼ teaspoon of garlic powder
- 6 tablespoons of shredded parmesan cheese

Method:

1. Chop up everything that needs to get cut up and place in the slow cooker except for the cheese

2. Stir well and put on high heat

3. Cook for about three and a half hours

4. Serve and enjoy with some of the shredded cheese on top

Nutritional Information:

Calories: 389 kcal, Fats: 23.6 grams, Carbohydrates: 25.8 grams, Protein: 21.8 grams

German Lentil Soup

Ingredients:

- 2 cups of brown lentils
- 3 cups of chicken broth
- 1 bay leaf
- 1 cup of carrots, chopped
- 1 cup of celery, chopped
- 1 cup of onion, chopped
- 1 teaspoon of Worcestershire sauce
- ½ teaspoon of garlic powder
- ¼ teaspoon of nutmeg
- 5 drops of hot sauce
- ¼ teaspoon of caraway seed
- ½ teaspoon of celery salt
- 1 tablespoon of parsley
- ½ teaspoon of pepper

Method:

1. Cut up everything that needs to get cut up

2. Place in the slow cooker and cook on high for about five hours

3. Remove the bay leaf

4. Serve and enjoy

Nutritional Information:

Calories: 221 kcal, Fats: 2.3 grams, Carbohydrates: 34.2 grams, Protein: 16 grams

Meatless Taco Soup

Ingredients:

- 1 onion, chopped
- 1 can of chili beans
- 1 can of kidney beans
- 1 can of corn
- 1 can of tomato sauce
- 2 cups of water
- 6 tomatoes, diced
- 2 green chili peppers
- 3 tablespoons of taco seasoning mix

Method:

1. Cut up everything that needs to be diced

2. Place in the slow cooker and stir well

3. Cook on high for about three and a half hours

4. Serve and enjoy, try with some sour cream and shredded cheese on top

Nutritional Information:

Calories: 362 kcal, Fats: 16.3 grams, Carbohydrates: 37.8 grams, Protein: 18.2 grams

Cabbage Soup

Ingredients:

- 2 tablespoons of vegetable oil
- 1 onion, chopped
- 5 cups of cabbage, chopped
- 2 cans of red kidney beans
- 2 cups of water
- 6 cups of tomato sauce
- 4 tablespoons of seasoned salt
- 1 ½ teaspoons of cumin
- 1 teaspoon of salt
- 1 teaspoon of pepper

Method:

1. Chop the cabbage and the onion up
2. Place in slow cooker with everything else
3. Cook on high for four hours
4. Serve and enjoy

Nutritional Information:

Calories: 211 kcal, Fats: 8.7 grams, Carbohydrates: 20.3 grams, Protein: 14.1 grams

Corn Chowder

Ingredients:

- 5 potatoes, peeled and cubed
- 2 onions, chopped
- 3 stalks of celery, chopped
- 1 can of whole kernel corn
- 2 tablespoons of butter
- ½ teaspoon of salt
- ½ teaspoon of pepper
- 2 tablespoons of seasoned salt
- 1 can of evaporated milk

Method:

1. Peel and cube the potatoes
2. Chop the onions and the celery
3. Combine everything in the slow cooker
4. Set on high heat and cook for about four hours
5. Serve and enjoy

Nutritional Information:

Calories: 266 kcal, Fats: 8.8 grams, Carbohydrates: 37.8 grams, Protein: 11.2 grams

Tofu Curry

Ingredients:

- 1 pound tofu (firm; cubed)
- 2 cup sweet corn
- 15 oz coconut milk
- ¼ cup curry paste
- 2 cups vegetable stock
- 6 oz tomato paste (canned)
- 1 yellow pepper (chopped)
- 1 red pepper (chopped)
- 1 sweet onion (chopped)
- 3 garlic cloves (minced)
- 2 ginger (minced)
- 1 tbsp garam masala
- 1 tsp low salt
- Cilantro (for garnishing)

Method:

1. Start by cutting the tofu into ½ inch cubes and add it to a large slow cooker.

2. Next add the chopped onion, peppers; ginger and garlic to the slow cooker as well followed by the corn, vegetable stock, tomato paste, coconut milk and spices.

3. Stir well! Then cover and allow the curry to cook on high heat for approximately 3 to 4 hours.

4. Serve over brown rice or as desired.

Nutritional Information:

Calories: 328 kcal, Fats: 7 grams, Carbohydrates: 53.8 grams, Protein: 12.8 grams

Overnight Oatmeal

Ingredients:

- 4 cups fat-free milk
- 4 cups water
- 2 cups steel-cut oats
- 1/3 cup raisins
- 1/3 cup dried cherries
- 1/3 cup dried apricots, chopped
- 1 teaspoon molasses
- 1 teaspoon cinnamon (or pumpkin pie spice)

Method:

1. In a slow cooker combine all of the ingredients. Turn heat to low.

2. Put the lid on and cook overnight for 8 to 9 hours.

3. Spoon into bowls and serve.

Nutrition Information:

Calories: 240kcal, fat: 2.5 g; carbohydrates: 47 g; protein: 11 g protein

Sauerkraut soup

Ingredients:

- 1 can of mushroom soup
- 1 can of chicken soup
- 2 ½ cups of water
- 4 cups of chicken broth
- ½ pound of sauerkraut
- 1 onion, diced
- 3 carrots, chopped
- 5 potatoes, peeled and diced
- 1 teaspoon of dill weed
- 1 teaspoon of garlic, minced
- ½ teaspoon of salt
- ½ teaspoon of pepper

Method:

1. Peel and dice the potatoes
2. Cut the carrots and the onions
3. Mince the garlic
4. Combine everything into the slow cooker

5.   Put on high heat and cook for four hours

6.   Serve and enjoy

Nutritional Information:

Calories: 387 kcal, Fats: 23.4 grams, Carbohydrates: 26.4 grams, Protein: 17.7 grams

Lima Bean Soup

Ingredients:

- 4 cups of lima beans
- 1 can of butter beans
- 2 potatoes, diced
- 2 stalks of celery, chopped
- 2 onions, chopped
- 3 carrots, sliced
- ¼ cup of butter
- ½ tablespoon of diced marjoram
- 1 teaspoon of salt
- ½ teaspoon of pepper
- 3 cans of vegetable broth

Method:

1. Dice and cut everything that needs to be cut up
2. Place in the slow cooker with everything else
3. Set on high for four hours
4. Serve and enjoy

Nutritional Information:

Calories: 326 kcal, Fats: 11.4 grams, Carbohydrates: 43.7 grams, Protein: 13 grams

Vegetarian Minestrone Soup

Ingredients:

- 6 cups of vegetable broth
- 4 tomatoes, diced
- 1 can of kidney beans
- 1 onion, chopped
- 2 stalks of celery, chopped
- 1 cup of green beans
- 1 zucchini, chopped
- 3 cloves of garlic, minced
- 1 tablespoon of parsley
- 1 ½ teaspoons of oregano
- 1 teaspoon of salt
- ¾ teaspoon of thyme
- ¼ teaspoon of pepper
- ½ cup of elbow noodles
- 4 cups of spinach, chopped
- ¼ cup of shredded parmesan cheese

Method:

1. Chop everything up that needs to get cut up

2. Place in the slow cooker with everything but the cheese

3. Put on high for four hours or so

4. Serve and enjoy with the cheese on top

Nutritional Information:

Calories: 138 kcal, Fats: 1.7 grams, Carbohydrates: 25.2 grams, Protein: 6.9 grams

Spicy Thai Soup

Ingredients:

- 5 cups of vegetable broth
- 1 cup of white wine(optional)
- 1 cup of water
- 1 yellow onion, chopped
- 3 green onions, chopped
- 4 carrots, chopped
- 4 stalks of celery, chopped
- ½ teaspoon of salt
- 1 teaspoon of pepper
- 1 tablespoon of curry powder
- ½ tablespoon of sage
- ½ teaspoon of seasoned salt
- ½ tablespoon of oregano
- 1 teaspoon of cayenne pepper
- 2 tablespoons of vegetable oil
- 1 chili pepper, seeded and chopped
- 1 box of rice noodles

Method:

1. Chop everything up that needs to get cut up

2.   Place in the slow cooker

3.   Cook on high for around five hours or until everything is tender

4.   Serve and enjoy

Nutritional Information:

Calories: 131 kcal, Fats: 3 grams, Carbohydrates: 14.5 grams, Protein: 7.9 grams

Lentil and Mushroom Stew

Ingredients:

- 2 quarts of vegetable broth
- 2 cups of mushrooms, sliced
- 1 ounce of shiitake mushrooms, chopped
- ¾ cup of uncooked pearl barley
- ¾ cup of lentils
- ¼ cup of onion flakes
- 2 teaspoons of minced garlic
- 2 teaspoons of pepper
- 3 bay leaves
- 1 teaspoon of basil
- 1 teaspoon of salt

Method:

1. Cut up everything and place in slow cooker
2. Stir well and cook on high heat for four hours
3. Remove bay leaves
4. Serve and enjoy

Nutritional Information:

Calories: 213 kcal, Fats: 1.2 grams, Carbohydrates: 43.9 grams, Protein: 8.4 grams

Pumpkin Goulash

Ingredients:

- 6 diced tomatoes
- 1 tablespoon of brown sugar(optional)
- 2 tablespoons of olive oil
- 1 onion, chopped
- 1 teaspoon of ginger
- 1 teaspoon of cinnamon
- 1 teaspoon of cumin
- 1 tablespoon of coriander
- 1 can of garbanzo beans
- 3 pounds of fresh pumpkin, peeled and cut into small chunks
- 1 teaspoon of salt
- 1 teaspoon of cornstarch
- ¼ cup of water

Method:

1. Peel and cut the pumpkin up
2. Chop up everything else that needs to get cut up
3. Place it all in the slow cooker

4.   Cook on high heat for about four hours

5.   Serve and enjoy

Nutritional Information:

Calories: 330 kcal, Fats: 7.9 grams, Carbohydrates: 37.2 grams, Protein: 28.4 grams

Thank you!

Here are some other titles that may be of interest to you from the Recipe Junkie family! All of these books are both in eBook and paperback format for your convenience. Many of these cookbooks have been and still are Amazon best sellers!

Email us to be put on the Recipe Junkies FREE newsletter list. recipejunkies1@gmail.com

Disclaimer: All rights reserved. No part of this book may be reproduced or transmitted in any form or by any means, electronic or mechanical including photocopying, recording or by any information storage and retrieval system, without written permission from the author, except for the inclusion of brief quotations in a review.

The information provided in this book is designed to provide helpful information on the subjects discussed. This book is not meant to be used, nor should it be used, to diagnose or treat any medical condition. For diagnosis or treatment of any medical problem, consult your own physician. The publisher and author are not responsible for any specific health or allergy needs that may require medical supervision and are not liable for any damages or negative consequences from any treatment, action, application or preparation, to any person reading or following the information in this book. References are provided for informational purposes only and do not constitute endorsement of any websites or other sources. Readers should be aware that the websites listed in this book may change.

Made in the USA
San Bernardino, CA
22 November 2015